D1716771

WRESTLING BIOGRAPHIES

DEAN AMBROSE:
THE LUNATIC FRINGE

TEDDY BORTH

abdopublishing.com

Published by Abdo Zoom, a division of ABDO, PO Box 398166, Minneapolis,
Minnesota 55439. Copyright © 2018 by Abdo Consulting Group, Inc. International
copyrights reserved in all countries. No part of this book may be reproduced in any form
without written permission from the publisher. Bolt!™ is a trademark and logo of Abdo Zoom.

Printed in the United States of America, North Mankato, Minnesota.
092017
012018

Photo Credits: AllWrestlingSuperstars.com, AP Images, Getty Images,
      Icon Sportswire, iStock, Newscom, Shutterstock, ©Anton Jackson CC BY-SA 2.0 p.12
Production Contributors: Kenny Abdo, Jennie Forsberg, Grace Hansen
Design Contributors: Dorothy Toth, Neil Klinepier

Publisher's Cataloging-in-Publication Data

Names: Borth, Teddy, author.
Title: Dean Ambrose: the lunatic fringe / by Teddy Borth.
Other titles: The lunatic fringe
Description: Minneapolis, Minnesota: Abdo Zoom, 2018. | Series: Wrestling
      biographies | Includes online resource and index.
Identifiers: LCCN 2017939289 | ISBN 9781532121081 (lib.bdg.)
      ISBN 9781532122200 (ebook) | ISBN 9781532122767 (Read-to-Me ebook)
Subjects: LCSH: Ambrose, Dean (Jonathan Good), d1985- --Juvenile literature.
      Wrestlers--Juvenile literature. | Biography--Juvenile literature.
Classification: DDC 796.812 [B]--dc23
LC record available at https://lccn.loc.gov/2017939289

TABLE OF CONTENTS

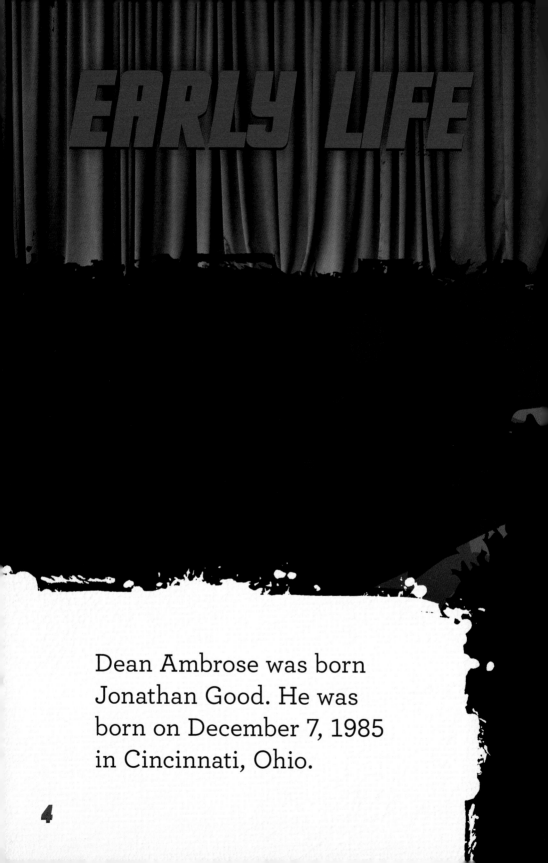

EARLY LIFE

Dean Ambrose was born
Jonathan Good. He was
born on December 7, 1985
in Cincinnati, Ohio.

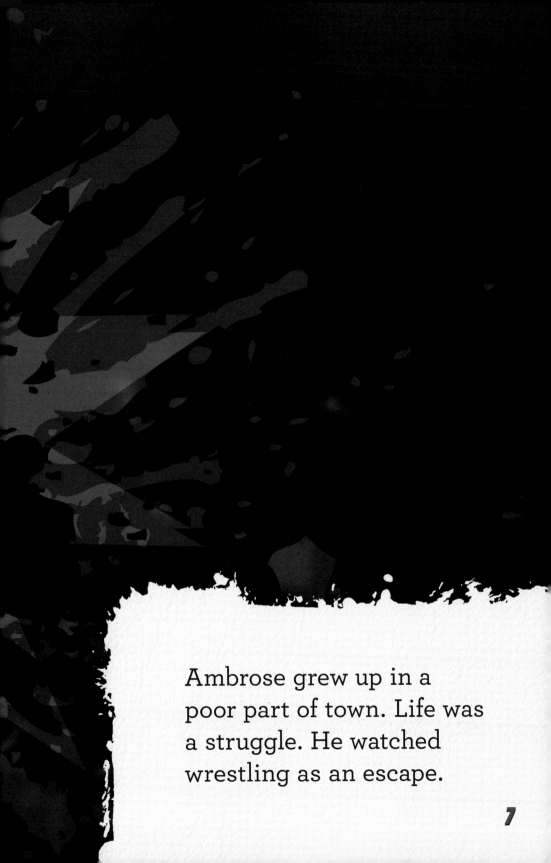

Ambrose grew up in a
poor part of town. Life was
a struggle. He watched
wrestling as an escape.

JON MOXLEY

Ambrose dropped out of high school to start training. In June 2004, he debuted as Jon Moxley. He started in Heartland Wrestling Association.

Moxley had matches for many different **promotions**. He won championships all over the country. By 2011, Moxley had the attention of the WWE.

Moxley joined Florida
Championship Wrestling.
He changed his name to
Dean Ambrose.

13

In 2012, Ambrose made it to WWE TV. He teamed with Seth Rollins and Roman Reigns forming The Shield. They debuted at **Survivor Series**. They were very popular with fans.

WWE CHAMPIONSHIP

In May 2013, Ambrose won his first WWE **title**. He was the United States Champion. Two years later, he won the Intercontinental Championship.

In 2016, Ambrose won **Money in the Bank**. This allowed him a **WWE Championship** match any time. He chose the very same night and won the **title**!

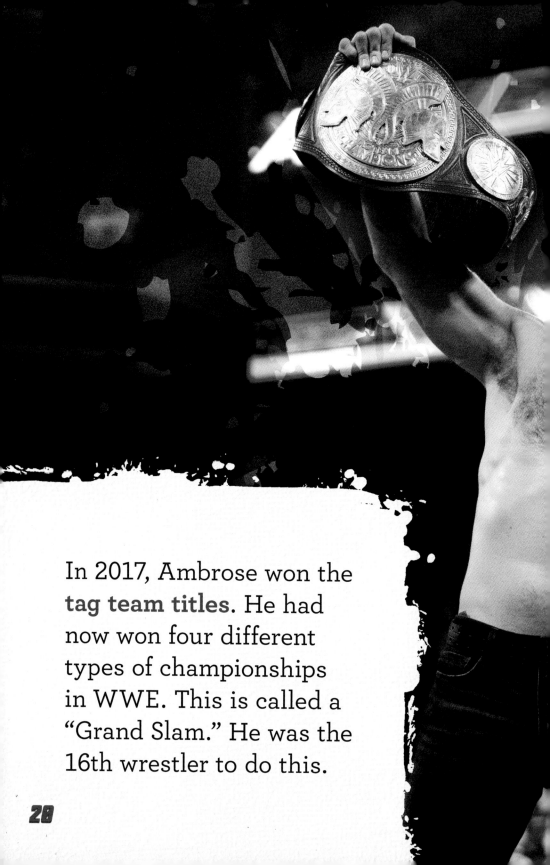

In 2017, Ambrose won the **tag team titles**. He had now won four different types of championships in WWE. This is called a "Grand Slam." He was the 16th wrestler to do this.

GLOSSARY

Money in the Bank – a type of match where a briefcase is suspended above the ring. The first wrestler to get the briefcase is awarded a contract.

promotion – in wrestling, a company that puts on regular wrestling shows. WWE, Ring of Honor, and Dragon Gate are examples of wrestling promotions.

Survivor Series – a major WWE show held every year in November.

tag team – a division made up of teams of two people. Wrestlers tag their partner to get in and out of the match.

title – championship; the position of being the best in that division.

WWE Championship – the top prize in WWE.

ONLINE RESOURCES

Booklinks
NONFICTION NETWORK
FREE! ONLINE NONFICTION RESOURCES

To learn more about Dean Ambrose, please visit **abdobooklinks.com**. These links are routinely monitored and updated to provide the most current information available.

INDEX